To The Principal
Yours Sincerely

SHANKAR MUSAFIR

Illustrations
RUSTAM VANIA

ISBN 978-93-81115-93-0
© **Text**   Shankar Musafir 2011
© **Cartoons** Rustam Vania

Illustrations Rustam Vania
Design   Mishta Roy, Bangalore
Printing   Repro India Pvt Ltd, Navi Mumbai

Published in India, 2011
BODY & SOUL BOOKS
An imprint of
LEADSTART PUBLISHING PVT LTD
Trade Centre, Level 1
Bandra Kurla Complex
Bandra (E), Mumbai 400 051, INDIA
T + 91 22 40700804   F +91 22 40700800
E info@leadstartcorp.com W www.leadstartcorp.com

US Office
Axis Corp
7845 E Oakbrook Circle
Madison, WI 53717, USA

All rights reserved worldwide
No part of this publication may be reproduced, stored in or introduced into a retrieval system, or transmitted, in any form, or by any means (electronic, mechanical, photocopying, recording or otherwise), without the prior permission of the Publisher. Any person who commits an unauthorized act in relation to this publication can be liable to criminal prosecution and civil claims for damages.

Disclaimer The views expressed in this book are those of the Author alone and do not purport to be those held by the Publishers.

To the educational
revolutionaries of India

Contents

Foreword by Abha Adams		5
Introduction		9
1.	The School as a Space	14
2.	School Events	22
3.	Experiments	36
4.	Questions	47
5.	Recess a.k.a Reflections	54
6.	The Principal	60
7.	The Library	67
8.	The School Community & Civil Society	74
9.	The Practical Period	82
10.	Art, The Art Teacher & Art Rooms	90
11.	School Outings & Exchanges	97
12.	Contextualising Mathematics	105
13.	Environment Education	112
14.	Quexaminations	120
15.	Education for Sustainable Development	128
16.	The Participatory School	135
Acknowledgements		143
About the Author		145

Foreword

In the midst of a dynamically evolving society, schools are the last domain to effect any change. Sadly, as educators, we know this only too well. Schools are bastions of tradition and dead habit and funnily enough this is something we are proud of!

Into this dreary scenario Shankar Musafir's book arrives with a much needed *mantra* – **let's reinvent!** He quotes from my favourite guru, Sir Ken Robinson, who says that reinventing and revolutionizing education is as important as climate change.

So welcome *To the Principal... Yours Sincerely*. The book abounds with ideas that truly contextualize learning experiences – from rain water harvesting, energy conservation to herbal gardens and **kabaad & jugaad** rooms.

Shankar brings the focus back to the child. Children are our *raison d'etre*, our 'reason to be'. Yet, while soldiering on with our school calendar, events and interminable functions, we lose sight of our children. Shankar gets you to sit up and question every activity and the way we do it. I loved the pot shot at our obsession with Annual Days. Who are they for? Certainly not the child!

To The Principal
Yours sincerely

I applaud his take on 'quizzing'. This will make us very unpopular but I have never understood our obsession with remembering trivia which can be resolved by Google!

Shankar covers all the spaces in the school. There are abundant ideas for meaningful and dynamic libraries; laboratories buzzing with action and art rooms and corridors alive with children's work. There is a plea for time – time for the children to reflect and infuse meaning into their life experiences.

I am delighted that he shares my belief that the school community of parents and grandparents is a vast untapped resource that could be mined for the benefit and advantage of all. The larger community is invited in and students learn from the experiences of workers and learn to connect with the legislature, judiciary and local government. This connect is essential for change. When connecting with the society they live in, they learn to make society accountable and drive change.

I fully endorse his plea for sharing good practice, ideas and innovation. We cannot continue to be islands unto ourselves. Schools need to come together and put their successful practices 'out there'. And we can do this now, thanks to technology. Consider how much stronger all of us would be if we pooled our experience and proven wisdom. Consider the impact it would have on children across the country!

To The Principal

Yours sincerely

Shankar saves his most radical idea for the last chapters – the Quexamination and the School Book! You have to read it! It would be unfair to reveal anymore at this stage. And as he closes with Education for Sustainable Development you know you are armed with the capacity to bring about so much change – and change not for the sake of it, but for a meaningful and relevant educational experience for our children – so that they grow up as rooted citizens, capable of making their world a better place with both courage and conviction – a natural outcome of their school life and education.

Abha Adams
New Delhi
June 2011

Introduction

Dear Principal,

After spending 15 years with school teachers during my school education, I have spent even more time with teachers while working with schools across India and the world. Being passionate about learning and teaching, I have had many interesting conversations with educationists and every time we talk about something important, the buck always stops with the Principal – the person who can really bring about change.

So, I thought of sharing my ideas with the Boss. Though primarily addressed to the Principal, all school teachers should be able to relate to this book, because it discusses at length their professional life.

I had shared a couple of chapters from this book with a teacher-friend and the first question she asked me in our

To The Principal
Yours sincerely

feedback meeting was, "Is this an attack on teachers? Do you want to shake them up?" While the answer to the first question is 'No', the response to the second may quite well be 'Yes'. How can I attack those who I love the most? And why not shake up someone, to make them come forward and take charge?

Let me share with you a little about the book before you jump in. This slim volume is about school education and reviews some interesting facets of school life, which, if reinvented, can bring about an enormous fillip in the pedagogic value of a school. And these facets are simple, like events in schools (Annual Day, Independence Day, etc.); the Principal's study; the art room; practicals; examinations; school outings and so on. This book does not emphasise theories of pedagogy but keeps it simple for the teacher, as well as for students.

This book is incomplete. You will find that I have missed a number of facets of school life, which may be more important than those which are in fact mentioned in the book. This is deliberate, as I did not wish to discuss issues of which I am ignorant. Only those areas which I have experience with and, more importantly, am passionate about, have been covered. So, do not expect the book to touch each and every important aspect of school life. Hence, I do not proclaim this to be a holistic book that can help you reinvent your school completely – but it is definitely a start.

Another incomplete area of this book is that it does not extensively discuss classroom teaching – a very important part of school life. The book is not theory heavy on pedagogy – rather, it is a platter of ideas on school education, which contextualizes the 'rituals' in a school.

While writing this book, I often recalled the rise of the Sufi and Bhakti movements during the medieval period in Indian history – the age when religions like Hinduism and Islam had become too ritualistic and people stopped seeing meaning in them... a major reason for the rise of Sufism and Bhaktism. It would appear that we are currently in a similar situation with respect to school education in India. There are a number of important things which have become rituals, taking us away from the true aim of education. Days and events in school do not inspire

To The Principal
Yours sincerely

children; practicals and laboratory work do not excite students to try out an experiment; and education has ceased to be a medium of change.

This book questions and jolts the rituals in a school and contextualizes them to make sense of them. I must also admit that this book is written with urban private schools (so called progressive schools), in mind and not so much with respect to Government schools. This is not due to my inclination but my experience as I have worked mostly with urban private schools. There is no denying, however, that the ideas are as much applicable to a government school as to a private school.

There are hundreds of innovative ideas around but when it comes to implementation, it has to be done by the teacher. Teachers today are a stressed lot. Apart from taking regular classes and checking notebooks, they also have to create reports, do household and school duties, take part in training, among many other things. With a minimum of 5-7 classes to teach every day and notebooks to check, it is quite a challenge if you are given additional responsibility in the name of innovation. I do understand that and hence have not proposed anything that would place an extra burden on teachers, rather it takes some off.

While the book is a critique of the present form of school education, it also moves one step further and offers solutions and ideas which do not cost anything. It offers simple ideas to reinvent spaces, themes and rituals, while empowering the teacher at the same time. It is perhaps quixotic at times, talking about things that are unimaginable in the school domain – about experiments not only in the classroom but at the school level.

So, if you are an action-oriented Principal or teacher, get ready to dig into adventurous ideas on school education. Do not take the sarcasm personally… I am on your side. But let us reinvent our world. As Sir Ken Robinson, the famous American educationist professes, '…reinventing and revolutionizing education is as important as fighting climate change in today's era.'

School as a Space

Dear Principal,

The school is an interesting space with clear-cut demarcations such as classrooms, laboratories, sports room, art room, playgrounds, office, etc. It is within this space that a child comprehends the meaning of education. A lot could be done to make this space interesting and pedagogically sound.

Building as Learning Aid or BALA, is one such effort, supported by the Governments nationally. BALA promotes customisation of the school infrastructure to aid learning. It is a series of hundreds of ideas on how this can be done, ranging from putting numbers on staircases, to using the sweep area of a door to teach angles. It is by far the best resource on using buildings as learning aids. And the beauty is that BALA ideas have been built in a participatory process, with teachers, architects and administrators all pitching in.

To The Principal
Yours sincerely

My effort here is to add on to this participatory space. Today, rainwater harvesting has been made mandatory for all school structures in most cities of India. Many existing schools too, have rainwater harvesting structures. Schools do announce this fact on their notice boards but the irony is that the students themselves do not have a clue about how and where the water is getting harvested. They just know that the school has rainwater harvesting. Rainwater harvesting structures can be easily customized for children to know more about this ecological imperative for the modern era.

The rainwater drainage pipes could easily be marked with arrows to show the direction in which the water flows when it rains. With little money spent, these drainage pipes could be brought to a single place where the water flow is easily visible to children when it rains (and before the water goes into the harvesting pit). While this may be difficult in existing schools, the schools presently under construction can definitely channelize water to a point in the courtyard or lobby of the school, where it could flow out of the mouth of an animal (or some other creative idea). Children would easily relate to rainwater harvesting with this method. Another commonly used tool is that of an inverted umbrella.

To The Principal
Yours sincerely

Moving further with the environmental theme, there is a lot of talk of children not switching off lights. Generations of Principals have given lectures on this in assemblies but nothing has happened. An idea, presented by a teacher from Ludhiana in one of my trainings, could well be the answer.

<u>To The Principal</u>

Yours sincerely

A digital electricity sub-meter needs to be put outside each classroom. At the beginning of the month, the readings will be noted. Imagine classes VIA and VIB side by side. The classes will be told that their readings are being noted and there will be a competition to see who consumes less electricity. You know what will happen after this – not only will it lead to more responsive children, but if the data is collected on a regular basis and collated, it could add value to the energy management system of the entire school.

Many schools plant beautiful flowers in their premises and to support the environmental cause, they also set up herb and vegetable gardens. However, the reality is that a number of students in the school, especially in urban areas, do not even know the common plants, let alone specific herbs. Many children have never seen a cucumber plant. So, while the child may somehow come to know about the Aloe Vera plant, s/he has no clue about the cucumber which s/he eats every day. The same goes for lady fingers, green peas and many fruits. So, it may be a good idea to have some lady finger plants in a pot along with flowers, leading to the school reception. The school can put a small placard there for the children to read.

This would be much more effective biodiversity education in a contextual manner. Although it sounds weird to put a plant of brinjals or peas near the reception, imagine the pedagogic value of the same.

For that matter, there could be trees of various fruits inside the school campus, so the students get an idea of what that grape vine (is it a tree?) looks like.

I have always been amused by a television show called *Crystal Maze*. In this game show, teams of individuals go through a series of hurdles to obtain a crystal. Sometimes they get into rooms and are required to undertake a simple assignment of throwing at a target or aiming at something. Why not have such outdoor games somewhere in the school, and which children can engage in during their free time?

Many schools spend extensively on technology and labs. A good idea would be to have a game in which, if the individual is successful, the machine shells out a toffee or some freebie. The children can engage in the game to learn something and would get rewarded for their effort.

To The Principal
Yours sincerely

There could be a corner in school which could be called the 'skill corner', where every day during recess, a skilled worker could engage children in the same. There could be a carpenter coming one day and a cobbler another day and so on. Interested children could just pitch in. A number of schools do such activities around children's day and PTMs (Parent-Teacher Meetings), but how about institutionalizing it?

More and more rooms are getting exclusive status in schools – the dance room, theatre room so on and so forth. Let me propose another room...the **kabaad–jugaad room** or the junk-innovation room. While *kabaad* refers to junk, *jugaad* refers to innovation. This would be the creativity room of the school, where all manner of things would be available, from screwdrivers to spanners, to springs, pulleys, kits to make radios, old mobile phones, radios, televisions, umbrellas, ball bearings, etc. The room would be almost like a mess with an invitation to children to create things and do whatever they want. While a number of students of physics do exercises on pulleys and springs, none of them actually see them in real life or create something with them.

To The Principal

Yours sincerely

Students could bring in their bicycles, skating boards and other such things and put them together to create whatever they want or need. Just like we have building blocks to let kids create whatever they wish. This would be an advanced version of the same for children to create something new. The children could even consider it as a place where they can repair their cycles.

If we were to visualize a school which churns out innovative products, then a *kabaaad-jugaad* laboratory is a necessity. Until such labs are created, which give freedom to children to innovate, we cannot expect new discoveries.

My father was an engineer and the toolbox with screwdrivers, spanners, pliers and other mechanical knick-knacks was always available. It was so much fun for me to sit with him and open some electronic equipment or repair something.

The beauty of this room would be that not only would it promote the environmental cause by using disposed things, it would also be a creative space of the school. Moreover, the school need not have this room specially

To The Principal
Yours sincerely

manufactured – it would, in fact, be the cheapest lab to be set up in the school. If manned by the right teacher and with ample safety precautions, this could well be the next Newton's lab of the school. Children coming out of these labs will give a hard time to professors at their engineering colleges. *Howzzat?*

School Events

Dear Principal,

I know the prestige of the school is of great concern to you and that is why you ensure that every event, be it earth day, annual day or any other such day, is celebrated with fanfare... I know you spend a great deal of time planning these events – with meetings, inspections, rescheduling, etc., and even more time spent in getting children prepared for the event – rehearsals for Saraswati *Vandana*, dances and everything else.

I also know that you have to get your speech ready in time for that big day so that the Principal's speech is the best part of the day. You have to also look for that right quote to put in. Plus, there is no denying the fact that the guest list for the functions often keeps you on your toes, especially if the Managing Trustee or his father is visiting as a special guest.

To The Principal
Yours sincerely

It's Independence Day.
Remember, No Talking,
No Running and Walk in Straight Lines!

On the day of the event, you ensure that the school turns out at its best. All the teachers are perhaps in their best attire (ensuring of course that they are not in the same clothes as worn at the last function), and wearing that new necklace which they would like the other teachers to discuss in the staff room.

To The Principal
Yours sincerely

No stone is left unturned in order for the event to be successful, and no doubt it is. I also had the same feeling until one day I realized something else… when I looked at a child sitting in the audience of a school event.

I could connect with him immediately. I wondered, as we were busily ensuring the success of the event…if that child had perhaps got left out? The Child – the person for whom the entire school system is meant to 'perform'. The children who are on the stage perform as usual… as they have been doing at many such events. But the entire school (read 'the students'), sitting in the auditorium, are getting bored. For them it is just another event…where everyone gets together, the Principal gives a speech and so does the Chief Guest, and finally everybody goes home.

The students are happy about just one thing – that they are not sitting in the classroom, getting bored. There are various forms and levels of boredom for a school student… and sitting in a classroom is higher up on the 'list of bores' when compared to sitting in a school function. Getting out of the classroom is the only novelty.

And then I looked at some of the teachers' concerned faces – teachers on their toes. I tried to read their minds and I was not too happy with that as well. I wondered what would be their most pressing concern at that event? It did not take much time to realize what their concerns were ... "Oh! My god...the bouquet has got only yellow roses and the Principal had asked for white ones...She is going to kill me!" Or "Heaven save me... I was supposed to put ribbons around the candles meant for lighting the lamp and I clean forgot!"

Over a period of time, I did this introspection at a number of school functions and have still to come across a teacher whose concern at the event is "Dear God...will this day touch, move and inspire the children about the 'issue of the day' [be it independence, the earth or what it may]?"

In ensuring the arrangements for your child's wedding and entertainment of the guests, you somehow forgot the one actually getting married. Naturally then, the child actually learns nothing about the day....whether it be dedicated to the ideas of independence, green earth or something else...

To The Principal
Yours sincerely

This prompted me to relook and reinvent at least one day out of the school's list of events. I chose Independence Day and it turned out to be a unique day.

While different schools celebrate annual days in different manners, it is not the same for Independence Day. The 'worst' school in the country, with ill trained teachers and an incompetent Principal, as well as the 'best' school, with the most motivated teachers and an innovative Principal, celebrates Independence Day in the same manner. They hoist the Indian flag, sing patriotic songs, or possibly have a fancy dress competition with the children turning out as Gandhi and Nehru. Some may go a step forward and do a play around Bhagat Singh's life. But essentially it is the same…whether it is a village or a city school, non-progressive or progressive.

As emphasized before, that small child sitting in the auditorium, or even the teenager, is not at all moved about the idea of independence by any of these events, despite the fact that the school has spent an enormous amount of time on rehersals and resources for the day.

Over a period of time, we have simply lost our focus on the child and become involved in various other peripheral things. The art teacher takes immense pains to do up the school with Indian flags and put up photos of Bhagat Singh et al, on all the notice boards... to bring the theme of independence to the school. The innovative art teacher perhaps hangs tricolour saris all over the school (to impress the Principal).

But that is not all...we have all become petty over a period of time. The Principal and her highly qualified staff, often spend the entire afternoon deciding on whether the guest should be welcomed with flowers or a shawl. Whether the photograph of Bhagat Singh and Gandhiji should be adorned with a fresh flower garland or the other 'long lasting' one? The music teacher is concerned with whether the patriotic group song should be sung wearing the school uniform or the more fancy *kurta pyjama* of pre-independence times...

And the chief guest...the father of the Managing Trustee... the Principal is most relieved to know in time that he is a diabetic and will thus have his tea without sugar. Sugar-free biscuits are then arranged.

To The Principal
Yours sincerely

Excuse the sarcasm, but as you see... everything has been taken care of...except the little child sitting in the auditorium. Nobody thinks what he/she will take home. Does this Independence Day celebration give him/her any taste of the independence movement? Is freedom something he understands? These questions are not difficult to answer.

So I started off on my own journey to reinvent Independence Day celebrations in school and began thinking about what we really relate to regarding independence... protests, freedom fighters, the Quit India movement, etc. What remains of the independence movement now? What came to my mind immediately were the freedom fighters and I knew that there would be some in every part of the country. Why not have my children actually go and meet the freedom fighters? Why not invite them to school to interact with our children?

So began my search for freedom fighters. I thought it would be easy to find them since many of them receive Government pensions. But it was far from easy. Obtaining the list of freedom fighters from the pension office was a travail in itself and eventually it did not happen (let's save that story for another day). So, finally I reached the office of the Freedom Fighters' Association of India at Jantar Mantar, New Delhi, and got the contacts of a few freedom fighters who lived in Delhi.

I must mention their names here as they blessed this project of mine. Subhadra Khosla was 13 when she was arrested in Lahore for taking part in the Quit India movement. An old lady now, she was the first person to actually ignite in me the energy to go on with the project. To my surprise, she was more than eager to meet the children. The same was the case with Hari Ram, who was 90 years old and an Indian National Army (INA) veteran.

The actual interactions of these people with the children, was an amazing experience. The children did not ask as many questions as I had expected them to, but they were visibly moved and so was the entire staff of the school, who also wanted to meet these freedom fighters. I will not go into the details of that interaction…but you can well imagine it. When was the last time you met someone who had actually fought for our country's freedom?

To The Principal
Yours sincerely

Another thing I did was to take the children to visit Jantar Mantar – not the monument but the road next to it… where people from all walks of life gather every day to 'protest'. People sing songs, shout slogans, go on aborted marches to Parliament House, or just sit there for a 'cause'. Interestingly, every day, there is one protest or the other taking place there. Since the independence movement also had different forms of protest, I thought the children would get a taste of this way of public protest.

The children were left at Jantar Mantar in groups and asked to interact with the protestors with a few questions in mind: Why are you protesting? What's your issue? Do you think this protest will have any effect? Why did you choose this form of protest?

So the children met the Bhopal protestors, some CPI (M) protestors against the Nuclear Liability Bill and a horde of protestors from the BJP, rallying against siphoning of SC/ST funds for the Commonwealth Games.

It is true that there were children in the group who found this exercise boring, but I am sure the experience will nevertheless remain etched in their minds for a while and may connect to some other experiences in life to create a learning experience.

In this entire exercise, the teachers were not stressed with extra responsibilities and the children minutely involved and interested. So, we managed to do a very nice school event with focus on the children and without the teachers getting bothered about bouquets and saris. In fact, a number of teachers walked up to say a word of thanks for the experience.

I should mention another sub-experiment within this larger experiment. A group of class 6 children were asked to write a letter to Mahatma Gandhi. No instructions were given to them whatsoever, apart from whom to address it to. The results were phenomenal – with the letters conveying so many different things. There was original thinking that went into the letters. One girl had written "…I heard everybody listened to you. How did everybody listen to you? Nobody listens to me in class…"

There were even letters starting with, "Dear Bapu, How do you do?" I was glad the children had started

To The Principal
Yours sincerely

connecting to Gandhi as a friend…and that gave me an idea for my next experiment around school events – Gandhi Jayanti on October 2.

Many teachers may imagine that I am criticising the event and promoting a project. Perhaps I am in a way. But my proposition is that instead of doing an event with just songs, dance and plays, why not also do something meaningful to engage the children with the issue at hand? Why not actually contextualise the day for the children by having them meet freedom fighters? Why not contextualize all days that we celebrate in school?

There is another aspect to note in this narrative. It could be that schools start inviting freedom fighters to school for Independence Day celebrations but still do all the things mentioned – lighting the lamp, speech, etc. With the result – the children will still get bored.

And here I want to draw the line… it would be much more worthwhile for a freedom fighter to go to a classroom and interact with 20 odd children, chat and take questions. That experience will remain with the children forever. All

To The Principal

Yours sincerely

the school has to do is to invite a few more freedom fighters to visit the school.

Similarly, we can invite the local Member of Parliament or M.L.A. to the school, not to give away prizes or to make speeches, but to speak in a classroom about the electoral system, elections and democracy. We will go into this in later chapters.

I am actually talking about making such days 'non-events' where teachers are not stressed about their saris and can concentrate on disseminating meaningful experiences to kids. I am talking about contextualizing events...wherein on earth day...*kabadiwalas* come to classrooms to talk about recycling.

Let's be innovative about days. And perhaps we have to start with the 'Annual Day'...because nobody actually knows why it's celebrated. It's just that there has to be one large celebration in the school every year... so we decided to have an 'annual day'. By that logic we should also look at starting something called a 'month day' and 'week day'!

To The Principal
Yours sincerely

Some progressive schools tweaked the logic and have now started calling it 'Founder's Day' though no one in the school has a clue as to who the founder was and why did he build the school instead of a factory. And mind it...there is no particular day when the school was founded...so it can happen on any day of the year...usually mid session. Or it could be that all founders 'found' their schools from September to November.

Thankfully we got independence from the British and we have something called Independence Day. Otherwise, we would have had to celebrate an 'Annual Day' for India and no Indian citizen would know why we celebrate 'Annual Day'. Or perhaps Diwali or Id (no religious connotations intended) would have been rechristened 'Annual day'.

One of the most innovative days in Indian schools is 'Teachers' Day', when a group of school seniors get to run the entire school. It's an experience for a child who is being taught and the child who has become the 'teacher'. But, sadly schools are viewing this day as a 'usual day'.

To The Principal
Yours sincerely

Nevertheless, if you interview 10 adults today to ask them about which 'day celebrations' they remember from their school life, 9 of them are likely to come up with memories of Teachers' Day. While there is still a lot of experimentation which can be done with Teachers' Day in its existing form, it nevertheless is an innovative day. Also, one of the reasons that even the teachers enjoy it is that there are no 'chief guests' to be entertained and no special saris required…it's a family function.

But then I wonder…do we require these guests or chief guests in school? Do they give any meaningful experience to the school? Hmm…

P.S. The last chief guest I invited to my school was a *Kabadiwala*. But that is another story.

Experiments

Dear Principal,

I still remember the day I graduated to grade 5...one of the changes I was excited about was the move from pencils to pens. I was now grown up and could write with a pen. Another thing which came in was a practical copy and a new entry on the timetable – Practicals. Now I could do 'practicals'... I could conduct experiments.

But it was a little too late. All the years until I reached grade 5, I had always wanted to experiment, had wanted to see what would happen if I mixed blue with silver as well as many other weird experiments which were never permitted. And now, suddenly the school said, 'you will do experiments'. But only those experiments which were in the text book – experiments of which the outcomes were already known. One then wonders... why did we do them?

To The Principal
Yours sincerely

EXPERIMENT LAB

Please follow rules strictly
- Silence Please
- Do not touch
- No Dreaming
- Be Cautious
- No Playing
- Follow Rules

To a child the very word 'experiment' is infused with a sense of adventure. Of thrill! Let us see what happens if...? Is it possible to...? But unfortunately, the moment a child is introduced to school practicals, experiments and the laboratory... the very first instruction s/he is given is not to experiment! Do not touch this! Do not touch that! Do only

To The Principal

Yours sincerely

what you are told to do. While I do understand that children may get into difficult situations in laboratories, nevertheless there are better ways of introducing them to labs.

There are so many inhibitions in engaging with the laboratory that the thrill of trying out an experiment dies away. The child is not permitted any free time to experiment on his/her own to let that seed of experimentation grow. Moreover, the laboratories are supposed to be clean, completely clean. I wish I could arrange a tour to the laboratories of an Edison or Newton and other scientists. I am sure they were anything but clean. And this obsession with cleanliness goes on unchecked in every school lab.

A practical 'copy' (read notebook), is an investment. This 'copy', bigger than the other 'copies', has a larger price too. It is a one of a kind 'copy' as one side is blank while the other has ruled lines. All you have to do in the practical copy is to write down the steps of an experiment on the right hand side (with the lines) and make a neat and clean diagram of the experiment on the other side. There should be no cancellations and corrections …it has to be neat and clean.

To The Principal

Yours sincerely

It is not difficult to imagine the practical 'copies' of Newton and Edison. There are of course the CBSE guidelines that need to be followed. But do you not think we have extrapolated the logic to the hilt? My Physics teacher at a school in Bangalore, Ms Usha, was perhaps the best teacher I have ever seen taking practicals. She was smart and made us do the right thing without violating the existing system of maintaining neat and clean practical copies. She advised us to maintain a rough copy along with the practical copy and then declared, "I will only check the rough copies".

We thought it was a joke but that was what she did. She never ever looked at our neat and clean practical copies but always checked our rough practical pages. She also used to say, "The dirtiest copy is the best... you have to work hard to get a dirty lab copy. The person must have done a real experiment to have done so many calculations."

I still remember one of the first experiments she gave us to do. We were in Class XI at the time and all set to do experiments on resistors in 'series' or in 'parallel'. But she knew where we came from – she gave us rulers and asked us to measure the tables and chairs in the lab, taking the measurements of laboratory tables at least thrice before noting them down. We wondered why. But we soon found we were getting different measurements every time we measured something! Then she asked us to take an average and thus taught us about errors in measurement... a learning we used in doing other experiments in the course. She was a great teacher. I don't know where she is now and whether she got the President's Award or not. But Usha Ma'm, you have got this student's award for Best Teacher. And I hope that every school has the good fortune to have a teacher like you.

You do not have to guess that our favourite hangout in the school was the Physics laboratory because we actually got to do experiments there. Usha Ma'm had given clear instructions to the lab-in-charge to let us take out any apparatus in the lab and do anything we wanted with it. We loved it and must have done hundreds of experiments which were not there in the book.

I dream of chemistry teachers who allow children to do harmless experiments before s/he starts teaching how to verify the cat ions and anions. I dream of a lab where students

To The Principal
Yours sincerely

are free to experiment. How I wish students would get excited about going to the lab to be 'scientists'. Laboratory – a place of freedom. Our obsession with labs as 'sacred places' with innumerable rituals, creates dumb children who keep doing experiments, the results of which are already known to the entire world and are in fact published. We kill the scientist in the child, then and there.

Another thing which I had been itching to write about can also be mentioned here. Science laboratories as I conceive them, ought to be interesting places, but I see no logic in them being exhibition areas. There is perhaps no science laboratory worth its salt in this country which does not have a human skeleton on display – some in boxes, lined with glass and some not (full of dust). Schools have spent considerable amounts in obtaining those skeletons.

But here is a very simple truth… most school teachers have never used it as an aid for an experiment…because it is not required. Also, no teacher would have ever spent even five minutes in front of the skeleton. Interestingly, none of the practical books from class 5 onwards, mentions the need to have a skeleton

To The Principal
Yours sincerely

present for experimenting...yet there it is in almost every science lab in our country. Have you ever wondered why?

The only sound reason someone gave me, was that it was used to teach the fact that the human body has 206 bones and the longest is the femur or something. So much of investment in order to provide that little piece of information... and where is the experiment? Laboratories, I am sure, are much more than exhibits.

On the subject of exhibits, many labs in this country have exhibits of star fish, some snakes and what not... which have no relation to the curriculum but are still there for two reasons:

1. What's a lab which does not 'look' like one? That is, a museum with exhibits which look 'scientific'.
2. After all, where else does the school spend its money given to set up a lab? How many beakers, jars and test tubes can you buy? Needless to say that there is no laboratory in this country, where students have not argued with the lab attendant to get extra test tubes. Test tubes are always a scarce commodity... with funds used perhaps to fund the star fish.

To The Principal

Yours sincerely

One would like to also meet the pedagogue who first said that 'practicals' and experiments should be introduced at Grade 5. Experiments have to be introduced at pre-school. And I am sure Maria Montessori would have agreed with me that the time when a child most wants to do experiments is in pre-school.

If one stops to think about it, there are so many experiments young children of Grades 1 - 5 would want to do – which would make education meaningful for them. Imagine a child who has been doing experiments since early childhood getting into a full fledged laboratory in college. S/he could well set the IIT/AIIMS laboratories on 'fire' with ideas and innovations!

The flow of thought on this issue led me to another interesting 'discovery' – there is no space in our curriculum for experiments in social sciences. While the sciences have been given their share of 'practicals' and now even Mathematics has its space, the social sciences have not yet been found worthy of having a lab.

To The Principal

Yours sincerely

Some pedagogues may question my intentions in experimentation in the area of social sciences, but it just requires a creative mind to do experiments in social sciences without compromising human dignity.

At the moment it is a challenge for any person to conceive of a Social Science Lab, but it will have much more than a globe. For innumerable years, children have wondered how glacial moraines, ox-bow lakes and for that matter, V- shaped valleys, look. But apart from some good expensive geography books, children have no clue what these features look like. Models on innumerable geographic features such as fjords, canyons, U-shaped valleys, could send children into an altogether different world of learning and information.

I remember going to my grandparents' house for my summer holidays, and there was a pipe leaking somewhere near the garden. My brother and I actually channelled that water into some flowerbeds down the hill. We even dammed the water at points and then let it flood. But it was interesting to see how, after some flow of water, the sand started collecting at certain places. The entire riverine dynamics of water was there in front of us. That was my geography lab as my school did not have one.

And why Geography… how about civics (I am glad somebody changed the name from civics to 'socio-political life' instead). Every civics book talks of the Constitution, but a child would have to go to the library to find a copy. How about having some posters of political parties, an Electric Voting Machine (EVM), forms used to fill nominations for elections (how many of us have seen them?), forms to get a water or electricity connection and so on. Hundreds of things come in when you think about it. And doing an experiment with all these things is not a difficult job for any average teacher.

Do I need to speak of History? Right from photocopies of original manuscripts to old newspapers, to actual voice recordings of speeches of Mahatma Gandhi and Jawaharlal Nehru, they are all available to be acquired and used.

Social sciences have a lot of scope on things to be experimented with. Children can go on to the streets and

To The Principal

Yours sincerely

collect data about what beggars feel about the government. It is equivalent to collecting data about measuring resistance around Ohm's law. If experiments in the sciences is a lot about data collection, then social sciences too offers plenty in terms of data to be collected.

The good news is that for a social sciences laboratory you need not get a human skeleton – a human being will do… be it a beggar, a politician, a doctor, a bureaucrat… that is something I will talk about in another section of this book.

Questions

Dear Principal,

Prof. Anil Sethi at NCERT, in a conversation with me, shared one of his observations about parenting, which has ramifications on pedagogy as well. He said that we often find parents asking 'scientific questions' to their children. He gave me an example, "Why does a *puri* swell when fried in oil and does not swell if it is fried in water?" or "Why is a rainbow formed?"

He told me about a friend of his in Bangalore, who has a 13-year-old daughter. Whenever he visited Bangalore, he would meet and talk to her. He would ask questions like, "Who are you?" And she would answer "I am a student." But then he would ask, "What kind of a student are you?" She would answer, "I am not a hard working student but a sincere student." Then he would ask what she meant by 'sincerity'. Once she answered the question on sincerity, he would ask,

To The Principal
Yours sincerely

"But aren't you a girl?" She would agree and he would counter question, "So does it mean that you are a 'sincere girl student'?" She would agree. Then he would ask, "Aren't you a Bangalorean?" She would say 'yes'. "But aren't you an Indian?" he would query to which she would answer, "I am an Indian as well." Then he would say, "So then who are you – a Bangalorean, an Indian or a girl student? Who are you?" With this dialogue, he would make the girl think. The girl confessed to her parents, "Anil Uncle asks very interesting questions!"

In the course of facilitating an Indo-Pak student exchange recently, I requested Prof. Krishna Kumar, former Director, NCERT, to do a session with the children. In one of the conversations/discussions it came out that 'Most Indians hate Pakistan but like the Pakistani people.' But then the point of discussion was, 'How are the Pakistani people different from Pakistan?' There was no answer to that. The discussion was left for the students to ponder over for themselves. It was food for thought for our kids on both sides of the border.

Getting back to my original point, we scarcely realize that most of the time the questions that we ask our children are scientific in nature. We never ask questions from the social sciences. Or let me put it this way – we never ask children questions about society. Here is an example: how many parents do you know who have asked their children any of these questions:

- ✓ Why does your mother work in the kitchen and your father does not?
- ✓ Why is the maid servant (read domestic help), poor, and we are not?
- ✓ Why is India corrupt?
- ✓ Why are there potholes on the roads?

We would rather ask scientific questions and if our children answer them right, we take pride that s/he is going to become a great person one day and solve India's problems. But one thing is sure, while the child may certainly grow up to find ways of frying a *puri* in water, s/he may never get the potholes on Indian roads filled.

Another interesting point to note is that we ask only questions to which we already have answers. Factual questions, with specific answers to specific questions. So, even if we ask a question based on the social sciences, it will be in the nature of, "Which year..." or "Who formed..." For instance, "Which year did Subhash Chandra Bose become the Congress President?" Or, "Who formed the Muslim League?".

But the beauty of the social sciences lies beyond facts. And while 'logic' in science is factual in nature (for instance, the logic behind the formation of a rainbow), the logic in the social sciences is not factual and is, in fact, to a great extent dynamic (for instance, the logic behind the failure of the revolt of 1857). Something, somewhere stops us from asking these illogical social science questions – the answers to which may vary and may not be known at all.

And since the fun of asking a question is in knowing the answer, we never ask questions regarding the social sciences because actually, we also do not know the answers to many of them. We never ask questions to which we do not have answers. And until we start asking questions to which we do not have answers, the human evolution of knowledge will at best be nil or slow. All that we will do is keep asking questions about what everybody already knows.

Nevertheless there are questions which make you think. So, in a way, asking non-factual social science questions can actually give some space for children to explore the answers and thus construct their own learning. Otherwise, all that we are doing is asking our children to become encyclopaedias – storehouses of all known information.

To The Principal
Yours sincerely

Encyclopaedias remind me of my own school days. The intelligent children were those who knew the capitals and currencies of all the countries of the world. They knew it all. And these children would answer at quizzes in a second. We all thought, 'Wow! What super intellectual people.' But I wonder now... is that intellect?

Jaya, a friend who is a theatre artist, discovered this fact and told me that if I needed some information, I should go to an encyclopaedia and search for it. Or of late, Google it. No super human was required. And even if a super human knows it all, how does that benefit society or for that matter, help the individual utilise his/her intellect? It is just data in a computer which has to be retrieved. There is no intellect and originality of thinking in being a quiz-whiz-kid.

Ever since, I have hated quizzes and I think it is the most archaic and underdeveloped form of activity human beings engage in (particularly in the field of education). Derek O'Brien and Siddharth Basu would definitely disagree. But no matter how much they try to convince me about quizzing being an analytic and reflex action activity, my opinion remains unchanged. At the end of the day it is

To The Principal

Yours sincerely

merely retrieval of data. Yes agreed! A P4 computer retrieves faster than a P3 one... but are we machines or humans? Certainly not machines... because we can ask questions and new questions get created inside us as old ones are answered.

Recess a.k.a reflections

Dear Principal,

It is a reality in life that everybody needs a break – to just sit back and see what's happening in life.

A normal school routine gives one a mid-day break, which children utilize to eat snacks and then get back into the study routine. A child studies various subjects during the day and is supposed to grasp many things. But the school gives no space for the child to actually think about what s/he is studying. Nobody asks what s/he liked during the day or didn't; what s/he in fact learnt. Instead, the child studies and studies all day and is then given more work to do at home.

If we look at our learning cycle, one experiences something (hear, touch, feel), reflects on it and then learns it. What happens in our schools is experience (primarily by listening to the teacher and sometimes through activities) and we expect the child to learn it...without giving him/her time to reflect on it.

If you ask any average adult today how much s/he remembers of what was taught in school, college or university, at the most it would be 10% of what was taught. This is because what they experienced in the classroom they did not reflect on and hence the learning was superficial and not absorbed into the mind. For learning to be concrete, reflection is integral.

To The Principal
Yours sincerely

The intention is to fill the child's mind with the maximum information/learning. How about spending two periods in just talking to the child and asking him/her what he/she learnt during the day? And actually giving him/her a pen and paper or some other device to express what was learnt. Give some time for reflection and then for the expression of that reflection.

How about calling this Reflection Period or *Aaj kya seekha?* (What did we learn today?) period. I am not talking about revising what was learnt today or recapping. Instead, leave the children on their own to reflect on what was learnt that day and what use is it for him/her.

A friend of mine who conducts parenting workshops said that most of the things that children enjoy are those that give them immediate pleasure. Be it games or eating or anything else. It is just the opposite with studies. We tell the child that you must study so that you have a great future. The problem is that the child cannot see and imagine the future and hence, does not get motivated to study. If only we were able to make the child realize that studying is fun…right here…right now, then interest would follow.

To The Principal
Yours sincerely

Reflection plays an important role here. Let the child reflect and figure out whether what s/he learnt is of any use. It does not matter if the child thinks that it is nonsense and s/he need not study. Remember, that is the truth for the child. But, once given this freedom, the child will spontaneously choose what s/he thinks is important in studies and do well in that.

In fact examinations should ideally be about reflection. Consider this. What if children, after studying for two months, are just given a sheet of paper and as their exam, were asked to write what they learnt from studying for those two months?

There is no question of failure in this… all you need to write is what you know and think of. You may even come across a child who writes nothing of what he studied and writes that studies are not worthwhile. At least the teacher knows what s/he wants in life, and other means of teaching the child could be explored. They just write what they want…what they reflect.

To The Principal
Yours sincerely

Taking this logic forward, the education system is a continuum right from KG 1 to Class 12 and then, one needs to immediately go into college. The system does not allow for a break or recess to actually sit back and see what one is doing in life.

I would like to propose that after 15 years of school education, it should be mandatory for students to take a break. They could either write a book on their school experience, that is reflect, or engage in an activity for pleasure and leisure… to allow them to look back at life.

An initiative called the Gap Year College, did something similar. After school, an NGO offered a time of reflection for school students in the hills. They got involved in local village projects and reflected on the aims and goals of life. They spent some time on skill building and a lot on what they actually wanted from life. It was a time to gain clarity on their aspirations and interests. They could then get on with whatever they wanted to do. Perhaps, we need more such gap year colleges.

To The Principal

Yours sincerely

Many people consider reflection a waste of time – it is not work. But, it is a supreme form of work, which only humans can do. Reflection can sort out many issues in people's lives and our education system. If there is a space within the education system for a child to reflect on what his/her interests are and what s/he wants, it would be valuable. Self-reflection is a key life-skill which needs to be a regular exercise for a child. Writing a diary is a key exercise in this. Many schools consciously do this by spending some circle time with the children in the morning, but more needs to be done.

In the senior classes, especially XI and XII, when students make career decisions, there needs to be sessions for them to reflect and question whether their choices are their own or influenced by their peers or society. The school counsellor can be a helpful resource in this exercise.

Perhaps Reflection is a more important exercise than prayer.

The Principal

Dear Principal,

Here I would like to express my thoughts about the most important person in the school - the Principal. Well, I know the most important person in the school is the child... but that is just the right thing to say. Everybody knows who the tiger is.

There are various things associated with a Principal – the first being his/her room, usually known as the Principal's Office. Generally it is a room which everybody – from child to teacher – would rather keep away from. Entering this room sends shivers down one's spine. The only people who are desperate to get into that room are parents. It is quite difficult for a parent to get into the Principal's room and actually get to meet the tiger. But unfortunately, access to the Principal's office is inversely proportional to your resistance to being there. So, while teachers are summoned at a moment's notice, parents wait for aeons to be summoned.

Let's have a look at the ambience of the Principal's Office. One common feature is obviously the trophies the school has won. Some Principals of the older schools have a special display area created outside the office for everybody

To The Principal
Yours sincerely

to view the trophies. But there are many Principals who have trophies displayed in their offices.

It is by far the largest room/office in the school. The Principal usually has a picture of Gandhi or some other national leader hanging on the wall. Another likely photograph would be of the Principal receiving an award from some recognizable personality. Interestingly, I have not seen any Principal's Office which has pictures of Maria Montessori or some other noted educationist, despite the fact that the school may be called the Play-in Montessori School.

A Principal's office is like a *sarkari* office, and does not give any clue to it being an educationist's office apart from the trophies. It is also interesting to note the conversations which take place in the Principal's Office. They range from admissions, to planning for events, to leave, to electricity bills, to welcoming the chief guest. Pedagogy or learning are the least talked about topics. Unfortunately, the Principal is also head of education administration and most of his/her time is taken with that.

To The Principal
Yours sincerely

But one needs to take a step back and ask, "What is the most important activity in the school?" I am sure 90% of the respondents would say, "Teaching and learning". Then by any logic, at least 90% of the conversations in the Principal's Office should be related to teaching and learning rather than anything else.

Many Principals would ask, "How will the school run if I don't do the admin work?" Well, there are many people, including the administration manager of the school, who can do some of those important things.

The Principal does the most important things in the school but misses out on the thing of utmost importance – teaching. Principals generally do not teach – it is considered an unnecessary job for the Principal. Interestingly, the number of classes one takes is inversely proportional to one's hierarchy in the school. If one has to teach less, one can be sure one is going up the ladder as teacher. I know of very few Principals who actually teach.

I happened to be at the Scindia School, Gwalior, a couple of years back for a workshop. The meeting with the

Principal, Mr Tiwari, was short and sweet. A while later, he passed me in the corridor with a duster and chalk in hand. I asked him, "Where to?" He replied, "Need to take the Chemistry class." That Principal, from one of the finest schools in the country, taught in the classroom. Later, he shared with me the information that he would not enjoy his work if he could not teach.

While writing this book, I made enquiries as to his whereabouts. He has, in fact, retired and taken on an administrative role in the Scindia Education Society. I got hold of a student newsletter in which he was interviewed after leaving. The last question was, "Which is the first place you would like to go to during your subsequent visits to Scindia school?" Mr Tiwari's answer was what I had guessed, "I would love to go to a classroom and teach." We need more Nirmal Tiwaris in our schools.

Another example is Mrs Puri of the Salwan Public School in Delhi. She also teaches English, if I am correct. But that's not the case everywhere as mentioned earlier. While Principals can and do give long lectures about teaching, they do not actually teach. They just go on rounds.

To The Principal
Yours sincerely

If the Principal is not in the office, s/he is on a round to see the kingdom... whether everyone is happy or not. It includes going to the primary section... coochy cooing and kissing some children and telling the teachers how dirty their classrooms are. In the senior section it means a little lecturing to the senior boys and berating some teachers for their classes making too much noise. And most importantly, summoning at least three teachers, one *mali*, two *ayahs* and one security guard, to his/her room.

Most Principals do not have the patience to sit through a class because I forgot to mention one important trait of the Principal – he/she needs to be talking wherever he/she is. Principals who listen are a rare breed.

Also, Principals rarely visit the 'war room' or the Staff Room. This is not an article from the hate Principal campaign, but I do wish our Principals were more involved in the teaching-learning processes considering that they are the ones calling the shots. Schools would deliver much better education if that was so. A Principal would be a lot better being like a call centre supervisor, who looks at all the Staff.

To The Principal

Yours sincerely

The Principal should be the best teacher in the school, someone who can lead by example, not just lectures. It is alright if he/she misses meeting a parent or a representative from accounts. That is not his/her job. It may be worthwhile for a school to recruit a parent counsellor-cum-manager as well. A Principal's Office, to my mind, should sound like a Staff Room... buzzing with action around children. I happened to be at the Principal's office at the Tagore International School, Vasant Vihar, Delhi. I liked the ambience. It was a small office and the atmosphere was casual – anyone could walk in. It smelled of action. My wish is for our Principals to be educationists and not just administrators.

The Library

Dear Principal,

The library is one place in the school which is sacrosanct. It is a place where children know they have to remain silent. All you can do there is sit and read book, silently. During my school days, one had to first requisition a book and only then could you read it. One could not simply go to a shelf and pick up a book, browse through it, and if you did not like it, go on to another one.

Things have changed a lot since then. Many schools now have open book stands where one can pick up the book of one's choice. But nevertheless, the library is not an exciting place for the average youngster. Many book reading sessions and book weeks are held in schools and perhaps it indicates the number of readers is also going up. But that does not really create an atmosphere for children to inculcate the habit of reading.

To The Principal
Yours sincerely

What else can we do to get our youngsters interested in reading?

Excuse me, where is the Library?

You are standing on it!

A good starting point would be to look at human behaviour. What makes a person go and pick up a book? If we were to generalize some of the triggers, they would be

To The Principal

Yours sincerely

somewhat like this: first, someone tells you that there is a episode in this book which is very interesting and you would like it. The anecdote sticks in some part of your mind and the next time you see the book, you pick it up. Second, if there is a film which releases (based on a book), everyone wants to read the book. Finally, it's a subject you are actually interested in.

We need to understand that book reading is essentially a personal activity and not a mass activity. You read a book because you enjoy it and like it. The only thing you could perhaps do to make a child read a book is to essentially get him interested in picking it up. Figure out the interests of the children and have books on those subjects available to them. We need to understand that an average child is not interested in reading, *Merchant of Venice* or *Oliver Twist*. He may want something like *Harry Potter* or *Hardy Boys*.

We generally consider the library as essentially a place for fiction literature. All the other books are subject related. But how about non-fiction literature for children?

To The Principal
Yours sincerely

Perhaps about making things, activities, adventure travel or something else?

How about a book on batting strokes (cricket) and bowling techniques being introduced to the children during their games class? There are hundreds of books on these areas which can be introduced right in the playground. In that sense, a librarian should not be stationary in the library. How about the librarian introducing Sunil Gavaskar's *Sunny Days* and a biography of Sachin Tendulkar on the sports field? How about the librarian introducing a book on drawing cartoons during art class? How about getting a field handbook of plants, trees and birds introduced to the children in the garden?

Some books may get destroyed in the process but it is well worth it. Because you may just find children going into the library to look for the book you introduced. There are many other ways one can think of as well.

We must also understand that most people do not get into book reading straight away. They start with readings newspapers and magazines, then short stories and

To The Principal
Yours sincerely

then get into serious reading. Libraries should be full of magazines for children rather than issues of *India Today* or *Outlook*. There are many magazines for children which struggle to stay in business. It is high time that school libraries gave them some patronage.

Let us have some young Indian writers come over and talk to the children on how they got into writing. I have yet to hear of any progressive school in this country having invited a teenage writer as speaker. While it is a good idea to invite Ruskin Bond as well, he is now an elderly man; why not give him a break and call upon a teenage writer. there are scores of them around.

How about cookery books in the Home Science Lab? Or a *Fun Experiments in Science* book in the Science Lab? Our history text books are mostly without pictures. How about getting some pictorial books with lots of vintage pictures of Gandhi, Bhagat Singh, etc. to make that history class interesting? It requires co-ordination with the history teacher, but really...is it asking for too much?

To The Principal

Yours sincerely

Justice Leila Seth recently wrote a book contextualizing the Preamble of the Indian Constitution for children as young as seven years of age. The book has a number of illustrations and is an interesting read. Such books could form part of the civics education in schools.

The display at the library could have books related to subjects ranging from sports to arts to history to civics.

Teaching glacial features in geography class is still a problem. Most text books do not have original pictures, perhaps the text book publishers cannot afford the copyright and reproduction fees. Getting some pictorial books from National Geographic can certainly help. And the children will keep coming back to the library for more.

Many schools also have literary clubs but they do tend to have boring reading sessions of some serious writers. There are enough stories of literary personalities in their text books. Let us not kill their reading instincts by giving them more such literature through the literary societies. Let them pick up books of their own choosing. Let's show them films based on books. A film and then a book introduction is a good idea.

To The Principal
Yours sincerely

Comics are another interesting way of introducing the reading habit. Children love comics. There are a number of publishers printing books on the French revolution, forest rights and so on. Graphic novels are also coming in. Perhaps it is best for a library to invest in comics and graphic novels rather than encyclopaedias which are rarely used but take up library budgets.

Librarian-teachers need to be recruited not just for their efficiency in library management but for how much interest they can create in children about books.

The School Community & Civil Society

Dear Principal,

A school community, in the general sense, includes school children and teachers. All the action happens with them. Parents and the community around the school, are not considered part of the 'school community'.

In the name of security, process etc, the school is isolated from the community. Parents are generally regarded as interference by the school. The only time they are welcome is when the Parents Teachers Meetings take place...which is normally just a platform to share results the parents already know and some minor feedback which tells them little about the progress and development of their child.

To The Principal
Yours sincerely

Parents, as any Principal or teacher will tell you, are a 'threat' to the school. Well, some parents are …in one sense or the other. But that should not be the premise to keep everyone out.

Parents are a resource which our schools have not been able to tap. In fact, it would not be wrong to say that a child, at any time, is either in 'school' or in 'home school'

(with their parents). Parents hold as much sway on the children as do the teachers in school. In that sense it is important for both to be on the same wavelength.

Parents are keen to be in the school but are usually kept off limits. How about celebrating a Parents' Day in the school...just like Teachers' Day? On Parents' Day, parents could be made to run the entire school. A group of around 100 parents could be chosen to do the job on the day. Not only will it bring variety into the classroom but also lead to innovations which have never been thought of.

Parents have a lot to share. Many would argue that parents may give out 'wrong information' and even 'contradictory information' to the children. But then, how many times have regular school teachers given wrong information to students?

There is a friend of mine who is contemplating the idea of using grandparents as a resource in schools, as teachers or in other roles (maybe just for story telling). In fact, Sir Ken Robinson, the famous US-based educationist, mentioned (on a TED talk), a similar experiment he was engaged in. Some of our schools do indeed have grandparent days, but what I suggest, is institutionalizing the community relation with the school…not as an event but as a regular activity.

Schools often organize career fairs and ask children to take certain tests for career counselling – but they have not been able to get into this particular groove yet. Speaking from a community angle, in the parents' list of any school, there are parents engaged in various professions and businesses – doctors, engineers, businessmen, army personnel, etc.

Why not select some of these parents to form a panel of career experts? A doctor parent could come over to a class and speak to the children about being in medicine. Similarly, this could be done with parents who are architects, businessmen, chartered accountants, etc. This knowledge, directly available from the person in the profession, is more valuable than what is offered by a career counsellor, who has to speak about all kind of professions at secondhand.

To The Principal
Yours sincerely

This could be a once-a-week event and the school could select a list of perhaps 50 parents from various professions to help out. The net outcome would be involved and satisfied parents, proud children and all of it gained at no cost to the school.

Moving on from parents, there are many ways in which a school can engage with civil society. Many schools call upon the local Member of Parliament or Deputy Commissioner, to give away prizes to students at their annual days. But is there a single school who has invited a a Member of Parliament to the school to speak about democracy, elections or for that matter, the Legislature pillars of the constitution? Why not call upon the local Deputy Commissioner to speak to the children about how the country's administration works? Once you start looking around, the school would find that almost every person in civil society can add value to the education being imparted at the school and thus become part of the school community. Right from the *kabadiwala* to the Municipal Councillor, there are people who are valuable resources for a school; they can do much better than giving a speech and handing over prizes.

To The Principal

Yours sincerely

I was a part of an experiment where the Republic Day celebrations in a school were being contextualized just by taking the help of civil society around us. As India adopted the Constitution on 26 January, we decided to contextualize the three pillars of the Constitution: the Executive, the Legislature and the Judiciary – on Republic Day. We decided to have a local judge (representative of the Judiciary), a local M.P. (representative of the Legislature) and the local Commissioner (representative of the Executive). All of them sat on a panel and spoke to the children about the three pillars and their relationship to each other. This was just a small exercise to engage community members and also bring meaning to the ritual of Republic Day celebrations. This is no-cost exercise which could be implemented in any part of the country.

We also plan to invite local representatives of political parties – not to speak about their party policies but to talk to the children about elections, canvassing, nomination papers et al. Local school teachers who have been part of election duties like polling and counting votes, could share their experiences.

<u>To The Principal</u>

<u>Yours sincerely</u>

I have been mulling over the idea of including in the education value additions from civil society, young people from colleges (professional and non-professional).. Recently, I was part of a project on entrepreneurship education in which students made business plans and executed them by setting up stalls in market places. As part of this exercise, we engaged students of the local Indian Institute of Management (IIM). Students from the entrepreneurship cell of IIM, Lucknow, visited the school as part of the project and interacted with the students, analysed their business plans and just had fun.

There is a particular way in which school adolescents relate to college students. They hold college students in awe. This was quite evident during this project. Just imagine if students from a Fine Arts college were to be given some time to interact with school students in a class, or for that matter, students from an engineering college come over to school and share their experiences of college with the students. The same experiment could be done with young students from MBBS, fashion designing, hotel management and others. It would make the school atmosphere vibrant and a dynamic learning space.

To The Principal

Yours sincerely

The utility of civil society is immense for schools. Prof. Krishna Kumar, once shared the information that the famous American educationist, John Dewey, had actually envisaged that every member of civil society should actually spend a couple of hours with students of a school, for a meaningful education. It is high time we implemented what he envisaged years ago.

While it is good for school children to go out to meet people, it is also time that the school opened its gates to civil society members to come in and be part of the education process for our children.

The Practical Period

Dear Principal,

The school teaches all manner of skills to children, but it often pains me when students of Grade 12 or recent graduates, look towards their parents to fill up forms for engineering or other college entrances. Students who later qualify in examinations for IIT and AIIMS, often get their forms filled by their parents. Students who know all the laws of thermodynamics do not know how to fill up a form and send a letter by registered post. Students hassle their parents to make bank drafts to be attached to their entrance forms. Why cannot the school system equip students with these basic skills – what we can term 'practical skills'?

This is the premise for my proposal to have a 'practical period' – when the school curriculum is dedicated to those mundane things of life which no academic syllabus caters to. Even one 'practical period' a month is good enough.

To The Principal
Yours sincerely

The 'Practical' Period!

Let's start with some basics. According to the Indian Constitution, every Indian above the age of 18 has a right to vote (i.e. have a say in electing the Government of India). However, most grade 12 students reaching the age of 18,

To The Principal
Yours sincerely

have no clue about voting. While the school takes pains to fill up the CBSE board forms of the students, nobody helps them to fill up forms to get an election identity card. How about schools creating a system where not only do the students (who cross the age of 18 in school), get to apply for an election I-card, but are also appraised of the political situation in the country?

Many educationists would argue about the validity of the idea of introducing politics at the school level. But just consider where we are going. Aside from this somewhat controversial idea there are other practical things, hundreds of issues, the school could help their students develop skills with.

I remember that I did not know how to get a cheque cashed or how to send a money order. I asked my father, who took out a hundred rupee note from his wallet and asked me to send him a money order. It was a learning experience for me to go to the post office, find the correct form to send a money order, fill it in and send the money order to my Dad. The exercise was simple yet empowering.

To The Principal
Yours sincerely

While the regular education system does teach a student how to write an application for sick leave from school, there are very few schools who teach students how to write an application to open a bank account or to present a complaint to the Municipal Commissioner about civic amenities. Perhaps a real life experience would be much better for a child, especially as numerous well educated adults continue to struggle with writing simple applications such as that required for getting a bank statement.

My father did an interesting experiment with me when I was in class VIII. He was in the Indian Air Force and was transferred from Delhi to a small place in West Bengal called Hasimara. There were only two schools in that small place; one was the Air Force School and the other a Kendriya Vidyalaya. I was all excited about joining a new school and making a new set of friends. Two days after our arrival, I was curious about when my admission process would start. So I asked my father. He thought about it and said, "Why don't you go to the school and take admission?" I was surprised and responded, "How can a child take admission? Parents are required." My father replied, "In which law is it written that parents need to accompany their children for admission?

To The Principal
Yours sincerely

All you need to do is fill up a form, fill up a few details like your name, age, etc., give an entrance test, pay the fee and that's it. You will require my signature. Just fill up the form and let me know where to sign. You don't require the parent."

Though initially scared, I decided to take it on. I reached the Air Force School and went to the office and told a staff member, "I want to take admission in your school." He asked, "Where are your parents?" I had all the answers ready. "My parents are required only to sign the form, which they will do. Please give me the form." After a little bit of a struggle, I was taken before the Principal of the school. I gave her the same answers. The bewildered Principal asked me my father's name and after a few more questions, told the office employee to give me a form.

Dad was right. The form was simple and for once I knew all the answers – my address, date of birth, previous school and so on. I filled it up and got it signed by my father. I gave the entrance test on my own, qualified, paid the fee and gained admission. The experience was extremely empowering. After Class VIII, I have always filled up all forms and all applications myself.

Another area which children venture into but are not supported by the school, is learning how to drive and applying for a learner's license. Most urban children are keen to learn driving around the age of 16 (when they are in class X). That is also the legal age to get a learner's license in India for riding a motor bike of 50cc and below. At the age of 18 years, one can apply for a permanent license. Why cannot the school help children to learn driving and actually teach them how to fill up a learner's license form? The school could also teach them some basic road signs to qualify for the test for a learner's license.

I understand there have been many cases of misuse of automobiles by teenagers, but then it is the same case with sex education as well. Just as our schools are coming out of the closet to conduct sex education sessions for children, why not driving lessons?

There are many practical things which could be taught once we start to think about it. Mrs Balachandran, ex-Principal of Ramjas School, R.K Puram, New Delhi, has been anchoring a programme called *Project Citizen* and she has actively encouraged children to file Right to Information (RTI) applications. While a number of adults do not know about the RTI process, these children are showing the way. A child who has learnt to file an RTI in school would go a long way in bringing about transparency in this country and the world.

Most of our school students do not know how to change the regulator of the gas cylinder or change a bulb in the house. How about this practical education? It could start from younger grades with classes on how to buy something from a shop. For senior classes, it could be how to book a train or flight ticket.

Though seemingly insignificant, these are aspects of life which are untouched and children learn through experience. While some people would argue that such things are taught by life, I would state, why not give them the experience right in school in an organized way? This could be clubbed with the now hot topic of disaster management. What to do in case of fire in the house or school? What to do if you feel uncomfortable with strangers? What to do if your parents do not reach school on time to pick you up? What to do if a snake bites you? Or for that matter, how to call the police or an ambulance.

Lesson plans could be made on some of the above topics or teachers experienced in these subjects can be asked to facilitate the classes. There could be hundreds of issues which could be tackled in a 'practical period'. It is time we have a period by that name.

Art, The Art Teacher & Art Rooms

Dear Principal,

The art teacher holds a very special place in a school as she has to be present on all the important occasions and decorate the school. Notice boards in the school are the responsibility of the art teacher. It doesn't matter if the children learn anything about art or not but the art room needs to look like an art gallery with all the good paintings and art work being displayed. The best art teacher is the one who is able to do up the school in a manner which makes the Principal happy and not in a manner that makes the child happy.

Most art teachers ask kids to draw something from a book or give them a theme to draw upon. We often forget that in the end, art is an expression…an expression of what we see, hear or experience. Rarely is the art taught in the class related to experiences. The teacher just announces that the children have to draw a market scene...out of the blue. So, at that moment...the kids just draw what they can remember of a market.

Art can be used as a very important medium of reflection, which adds value to what has been learnt in a variety of subjects. So, if the children come back from a visit to a museum, in their next class the teacher should ask them to reflect about their visit to the museum and then draw their reflection.

To The Principal
Yours sincerely

A number of inferences about the learning of kids could be drawn from what they draw. Remember the drawing in the famous film 'Taare Zameen Par'. When Aamir Khan flips through the pages of the drawing of the family of the child, he finds that the distance between him and the family is growing…a direct reflection of him being sent to boarding school.

So, after teaching a chapter on the Mughal period, if a history teacher just takes the help of the art teacher and asks the children how they visualize the Mughal period, children could draw hundreds of things, which the history teacher never imagined. The same could be done after teaching a short story in English or Hindi literature. Children could be asked to draw a scene from the short story, they could imagine clearly.

I know I am talking about integration in one sense now and a lot of schools do not give the space to teachers from different subjects to integrate. But tell me, if a history teacher just informs an art teacher that she just taught Ashoka and she could perhaps use it as a theme in the art class, it won't take even a minute to communicate this.

To The Principal
Yours sincerely

Imagine if these paintings are put on display in the classroom; the classroom would become an exhibition for anyone to learn about the Mughals or Ashoka, whatever the case may be.

A lot of people would argue that it may become a thematic overload on a student to be doing history even in the art class. I totally agree and would hence recommend this exercise only a few times a year.

It could also be done as an alternative to a written examination for a chapter. The CCE recommends alternative modes of assessment. It says, *'Use a variety of ways to collect information about the learner's learning and progress in subjects and cross curricular boundaries.*[1]*'*

Children could be asked to paint their learnings from a particular chapter instead of conducting a written examination. Believe me, children would love it and may get more interested in the issue. I met a Vice-Principal of a school and she shared that the greatest problem with FA or Formative Assessment in CCE is that the test cannot be written. Well…here's the answer then.

---

[1] CCE Teachers' Manual, CBSE, 2010 pg 7

To The Principal
Yours sincerely

Coming back to imagining real experiences, just after the summer break, kids could be painting experiences of their holidays. Plan International, an NGO did something similar when it made children across India draw about child abuse. Now it is doing a research on what insights can be gained from the drawings about the scenario of child abuse in India.

Moving on, instead of just sitting in a classroom and providing children with topics, a good idea would be to go to the school playground and ask the children to draw what action they see there.

If the above happens, a lot of children with an artistic bent of mind would start expressing themselves through their paintings, illustrations or some other pictorial form.

We need to understand that while languages give the students access to expression through words (read language), art gives access to students to express through alternative means.

To The Principal
Yours sincerely

Human beings primarily express through language, art or action. If the school provides ample means to let children express in all these three, it will lead to a holistic development of the child. Unfortunately, the primary mode of expression allowed in schools is language and true expression is suppressed even there.

Let me move on and talk about the key responsibility area of an art teacher - the notice board. Art teachers are supposed to create colourful notice boards at least in the junior section. Even in the senior section, often the art teacher is held accountable for the aesthetics of the notice boards.

While good looking notice boards may add to the value of the school and one may be able to impress visitors to the school, it may be worthwhile to give some time out to the art teacher to go out and explore art in various other rooms and classes.

Why don't we let students decorate the school? They may not do as good a job as the art teacher, but if it frees up her time and increases students' interest in art, why not? I

To The Principal
Yours sincerely

would love to visit a school with average notice boards done by children, which are genuinely expressive in art form.

Moreover, art is perhaps the most difficult subject to teach to kids. The Art teacher should be relieved of all 'decorable' duties to devote her time to generating the students' interest in art. It is better to have an averagely decorated school with students interested in art rather than a lavishly decorated school with students hating art classes.

School Outings & Exchanges

Dear Principal,

Every year the school takes the children to some interesting places in the name of 'educational trips' and some honestly call them 'exposure trips'. Trips are useful tools to bring about change in the usual school routine. In fact, a number of private companies have sprung up, providing quality, facilitated tours for children who often learn a lot from such tours.

Most of these tours are to some outdoor places where some action could happen. A recent trend has been exposure visits of urban students to villages to understand village economy and society. Pravah, a non-governmental organization started this trend and has by far the best village excursion for students. Clubbed with life-skills workshops, it gives a fair view of developmental work happening in villages.

There have also been a number of international exchange programmes with tie-ups with schools in the UK and USA. Let me add a few more elements and options to these outings and exchanges. While IITs and medical colleges are in the wish-list of many an aspiring student, very few students actually visit the campuses of these institutions. Not many schools in Delhi, Mumbai or Chennai take their children to visit the local IIT. It could have a great impact on children. Imagine first year engineering graduates taking Class XI children on a tour of the campus. It would be an altogether different experience.

These visits could be a regular part of the school's activity. For example, all Class XII students in Delhi, could be taken on a tour of the colleges of Delhi University (Arts, Fine Arts, Commerce, Fashion Design, Law and Science, engineering, medicine). Children can learn a lot from these tours and devoting a couple of days to this would certainly not be a waste of time for Class XII children.

To The Principal
Yours sincerely

I don't see the point of this trip!!?

Another emerging trend is student tours to Europe, the US and South East Asia. While I am not against these tours, I do wonder what stops us from visiting countries in the South Asian region. A visit to Pakistan for an Indian child would actually aid conflict resolution rather than a trip to Bangkok. Trips to Bangladesh, Nepal, Bhutan and Sri Lanka, could also be considered. Exchange programmes between culturally similar countries make much more sense than countries which have very dissimilar cultural and social contexts. A number of projects could be implemented in South Asian countries and the results shared. Best practices would be implemented with minimal customization. Let me also add that trips within South Asia are more economically viable than trips to the US or Europe.

I happened to travel with a child on a trip to Norway and he enjoyed it very much. A few months down the line, the same child travelled with me to Lahore, Pakistan. The child did not want to come back from Lahore and shared that he had learnt much more visiting Pakistan. He had a lot to say. It is true that we have a lot to learn from developed countries, but 'south-south co-operation and collaboration' is also important.

Even for trips to developed countries, a developmental angle could be added. Eminent non-profit, Voluntary Services Overseas (VSO) conducts trips where groups of youngsters from a developing and developed country spends time together first in an Indian village and then in a British village. We could look at similar programmes where Indian students visit villages in Europe and the US. Alternatively, they could meet the poor and the homeless in Europe and the US and find out why they are still in poverty despite prosperity in their country. Engaging in discussions on developmental issues on such trips could make them more meaningful.

NASA trips are getting popular with high end schools but how about an ISRO trip – the point being that there has to be a balanced approach towards outings – which should be a judicious mix of developed and developing countries.

These so called educational trips are non-subject specific and do not really match the aim of education. Children enjoy them just because they get a chance to be outside the classroom. How about subject specific trips?

I do not know of any school in India which has taken children to see V-shaped valleys or gorges or ox-bow lakes or glacial moraines or deciduous and coniferous forests as a Geography trip. While a school trip may be arranged from Delhi to Jaipur to show the children the fort, the entire geography of this region, seen in the fields and villages along the Delhi-Jaipur highway, is missed. The entire chapter on *jowar*, *bajra*, *rabi* and *kharif* crops is bypassed.

Children from as far away as Mumbai visit Darjeeling on school trips but how about taking them for a trip to Jaduguda or the Jhunjhunu mines or the Bokaro Steel Plant, all of which they have to mark on a map for their Geography examinations? Why not take children to visit Sambhar Lake, Neyveli or Durgapur – names we have all heard of but never visited. A trip to these places may very well be more worthwhile than spending lakhs on that trip to NASA. The north-east should definitely score over NASA for many reasons.

Talking about science, apart from the museums, why not conduct trips to the Indian Institute of Science, DRDO, IARI Pusa, Bhabha Atomic Power Plant, ISRO, Forest Research Institute, IITs and AIIMS? For sports, visits could be organized to hockey federation camps, shooting ranges, wrestling and boxing schools from Haryana, and round the year camps.

We talk about the Panchayati Raj System but how many children have actually met a *Gram Pradhan* or been to a *Gram Panchayat* meeting? How many children have met the members of a *Zila Parishad* or BDO to understand the structure? While children are often taken to Parliament and the *Vidhan Sabha*, nobody takes them to the Election Commission of India.

Every year, some state or the other goes to the polls; why not take the children on a visit to a state where elections are being held – to see democracy in action – the canvassing, hanging of posters, filling in of nomination forms, the polling and counting of votes? How many children have been to a polling station on polling day?

My submission is to conduct at least one such out-of-the-box outing for children in the year. Also, it is high time we stopped taking children to factories. I know they enjoy visiting an ice-cream or cold drinks factory because they get some good things to sample, but there is very little to learn

To The Principal
Yours sincerely

from full fledged factories with machines. It may be more worthwhile to take the children to a local cobbler or carpenter and let them see him at work. With the requisite safety precautions, the construction site of a building is another interesting place to explore, with masons at work, plastering or laying bricks or scaffolding the roof. Facilitated interactions with construction workers from poor villages can open avenues of thought for this country to change. Meeting supervisors and architects, who show the entire plan of the building, would go a long way to grow a child's knowledge.

Public works in progress are interesting places to be in. During my childhood and even now, it is amusing to see a JCB dig up a place or a road being laid. You often find hordes of people looking at the JCB at work. Remember the film, *Taare Zameen Par*; there are few scenes where the child actually stops to look at such work in progress, even a house being painted. These are places where the imagination of a child increases phenomenally. Even things as small as a painter at work can rejuvenate a child as much as an adult.

Though seemingly a minor matter, these visits can alter the thinking of a child and put his knowledge in perspective.

Contextualising Mathematics

Dear Principal,

What I write now may be more relevant to mathematics teachers rather than to the Principal, but nevertheless, the Principal should always be an inspiration for teachers.

Mathematics is a weird subject – in the sense that it is a tool, an aid, and yet a subject. While language is also a tool and an aid, the advent of literature and poetry adds life to it. A language by itself is just grammar – it does not have soul until it manifests as a story or a poem.

That is why I call mathematics 'weird' – because it is nothing more than grammar. Mathematics does not have a soul of its own. Its soul can only be felt if it is manifested by application in real life. That is the sad part – that the actual

To The Principal
Yours sincerely

application of mathematics in real life is missing in the curriculum. That is precisely the reason millions of students across the world hate maths. Text books present it as a tool with people being asked to practice it again and again. Imagine if English and Hindi were just taught as grammar with people practicing verbs, adverbs and adjectives again and again. Students would start hating language subjects if that were the case.

'...but we Indians invented ZERO, right?'

To The Principal
Yours sincerely

As long as the question is: $2x + 4y = 100$, it is difficult to answer for a child. But as soon as it becomes twice Rahul's age plus four times Vipin's age is 100, the question starts to make sense as it gets real life application and soul. I have always enjoyed questions of that nature.

Maths has been predominantly done on paper. Of late, Maths labs have been introduced, but they also consist of gadgets which make Maths more like a tool than reality. Also, the possibility of a Maths teacher taking the children out of the classroom, is less. As long as Maths remains on paper and the so called Maths labs, it is going to be the most hated subject around.

Jharna De, a maths teacher and a good friend, believes that Maths is everywhere. Then why do we not take children everywhere? Finding the mileage while travelling in a car; while selling *kabadi* to the *kabadiwala*, or while purchasing something…

Here is a practical example: when volume is introduced in the classroom and children are taught the volume of a cylinder, what stops a teacher from taking the children to a cylindrical tank? These days almost all water

To The Principal
Yours sincerely

tanks are cylindrical. The children can take a measuring tape along and note the dimensions and do pie r square h. I asked an office colleague the volume of a cylinder and she was not able to give me the formula. The reason is simple, the Maths teacher in her school did not put soul into the formula.

Similarly, while teaching mensuration, I hardly know of any schools where the Maths teacher takes the children out to the playground and asks them to measure the area of the playing field or of the classroom or corridor.

Most of you will remember the problem of the ladder on the wall in Trigonometry. A ladder is put against the wall and one knows the distance of the ladder from the wall and its angle. You use the tan theta (perpendicular by base) to find the height of the ladder. It is not hard to find a ladder in a school. How about actually putting it against the wall, creating a problem and solving it? It is entirely possible that the students will never forget the formula or how to go about it.

Similar exercises need to be done to measure the height of trees or other things. Rather than doing the same exercise on paper, if it is done for real, it helps.

To The Principal

Yours sincerely

The following quote from the CCE document (Continuous and Comprehensive Evaluation) of CBSE is relevant:

We assess learners basically on examination results, we do not assess effort, performance, attitudes to learning, ability to practically apply what is learned in every day situations, nor do we assess them on how creatively they use techniques or critically evaluate different theories[1].

One could integrate the above exercises with CCE by taking a test of volume measurement of a cylinder or measuring the area of a playground by actually giving a measuring tape to a child. It will be an assessment of the 'ability to practically apply what is learned in every day situations'. The same could be done with the ladder. It is only with these ideas that the non-written evaluation recommended in CCE will come into practice.

Coming back to the ladder, perhaps there could be a corner in the school, where a ladder is placed every day, at varying heights, for children to solve problems. There are hundreds of other ways in which the building of the school could be used to aid Mathematics.

---

[1] CCE Teachers Manual, CBSE, 2010, pg.6

Building as a Learning Aid or BALA, initiated by Kabir Bajpai, has a number of examples to make the school space into a learning environment. I have written about it in another section of this book. Questions like two cars starting from point A and B at varying speeds could be enacted with cycles in the school playground. The same could be done for a number of problems in other fields of mathematics.

In the environmental auditing programme of the Centre for Science and Environment, we had an exercise to find the total water consumption of a school. While it was easy to find the litres of water from the municipality (it was mentioned in the bill), it was a challenge to find the amount of water used by the sprinkler on the lawns – it was directly connected to the underground water pump.

We did a simple exercise. We took a bucket of water and found its volume (20 litres). We put the underground water pump on and put the pipe in the bucket. We noted the time in which the 20 litre bucket filled up. It was 30 seconds. So, 40 litres in a minute. All that we had to do to find the volume of water used was to find how many minutes the pump was put on for sprinkling. This was done in

To The Principal

Yours sincerely

thousands of schools across the country and I am sure they will remember it for life.

A lot has been written on using playing cards, monopoly (business) and other games for Maths. Playing cards and monopoly are directly relevant games to introduce Mathematics to children.

There could be hundreds of other such examples. The point is to bring back soul into Mathematics and connect it to real life and spend time on real life experiments of Mathematics. If a little thought is given, even differentiation and integration can be contextualized for children.

Environment Education

Dear Principal,

Schools are actively participating in the environmental movement in the country. Almost every school celebrates environment day and conducts debates/declamations or at least has a painting competition based on the environment. Each school does its bit on environment education. The more proactive schools take out rallies or 'greenathons' where students with placards go around the community shouting slogans to plant trees. Some even talk about saving water and electricity.

The end result is a group of students who talk about planting trees and saving water as an answer to all environmental problems. But how does one save water? Nobody knows. It is just feels good to talk about the environment. The trees planted at these rallies do not survive a fortnight. The very students who planted the trees never

To The Principal
Yours sincerely

visit the site again. As far as the school goes, almost every space on the premises is planted and there is no space for further planting.

Students talk about tigers being killed and forests being cut...they write essays on it...debate it...create paintings about it. But all this talk of the environment is 'out there' for them – something unrelated to their day-to-day lives. All of this environmental degradation happens at a distant location over which they have no control, yet they talk about it while being dropped to their schools by their chauffeurs.

There is another genre of schools with rainwater harvesting and water recycling structures – they tie up with some well known NGO and put up a board outside the school stating that the school has all the latest features. But the reality is that none of the students in the school have a clue about what is going on.

The reality is that true environment education, which makes students realize that even the water that they drink is a part of the environment, is missing. The term 'environment' for a student simply means putting litter into a dustbin and forgetting about it after that.

Another fad related to the environment, at least in northern India, is the 'anti-cracker' one. Hundreds of schools have joined this campaign, doing street plays etc. It is a campaign to enrol other students into not using crackers. Burning crackers on a single day, on Diwali, it seems is more harmful to the environment than using a car every day of the year. The fun a student could have on one day in the year is compromised. There is no talk of minimizing fire cracker use, but only stopping it. It would perhaps be more worthwhile for schools to invest in enrolling students to stop using personal transport or start granting admission to students who live near the school.

The hypocrisy is so widespread that while schools profess proudly that they have vermi-composting, there is no effort to take the initiative to the homes of the children. Paper recycling is only for demonstration purposes and the people who put tonnes of paper into the recycling channel (the *kabadiwalas*), are nowhere to be seen or acknowledged.

I was part of an environmental auditing programme of schools, anchored by the famous Centre for Science and Environment. It was amazing to see that the schools were comfortable doing their skits and rallies on the environment but shied away from actually getting down to the brass tacks by finding out per capita consumptions of water and energy. It took a lot of effort to convince the schools to get realistic about the environment and start looking at it in terms of usage of resources. But still there are many schools that are happy with rituals rather than rigour.

All the above may not make sense to an average teacher but there is no denying the fact that the human element is externalized in the entire environmental movement in schools.

While there is talk of waste management, there is hardly a school where the housekeeping staff works along with the children to undertake active waste management. There is talk of biodiversity but the school *mali* or gardener is external to it. There are hardly any students taking advantage of the local knowledge of biodiversity utilising the gardener's knowledge. There are people manning the paper recycling plant in a school but the students do not relate to it. People from the informal recycling industry like the *kabadiwalas* and rag pickers, have no space in the environmental movement in schools.

This is precisely the reason why the children can write essays on climate change and do declamations on global warming and have painting competitions on

To The Principal
Yours sincerely

environmental pollution, but cannot create action in their real lives. Environmental activism has become a ritual in schools. Schools set up herbal gardens with support from NGOs and the government, but nobody knows how these herbs relate to real life.

We did an experiment wherein we tried to bring in the human element in a project around herbal gardens. An NGO approached the school to set up a herbal garden. Before starting, we decided to make the children explore their own kitchens to find what herbs were available there, including *ajwain*, ginger and garlic. Later, the children explored the availability of herbal products in the local shops and compared the prices of herbal products with cosmetic products. An exhibition of herbal products was done in the classroom.

In addition, the school visited the Department of Unani Medicine at Jamia Hamdard University, where they met a *Hakeem* or practitioner of Unani medicine. We could have even met a *Vaid* (Ayurvedic healer) or an *Amchi* (a Tibetan medicine healer). All this put the herbal garden in perspective and gave the children a taste of real, traditional medicines and herbs.

To The Principal

Yours sincerely

It was after all this that the herbal garden was set up. Planting herbs made more sense after this rather than the usual affair of setting up the garden and naming the plants. It is these diverse elements that schools need to explore while getting into an environmental project.

Similarly, the human element needs to be introduced within water projects, involving the school plumber, local municipality officials, officials of sewage treatment plants, fishermen, boatmen, etc. In energy projects, by involving the school electrician, the administrative manager and the local Electricity Board officials. In afforestation programmes, by meeting the forest officials, lumberjacks, professionals in the furniture industry and carpenters. In e-waste projects, by meeting the manufacturers, collectors, users and local store owners. This would prove to be more helpful than *greenathons*, rallies, painting and essay competitions and declamations.

Meaningful environmental projects involve the human element and let environment education be a live project rather than just an academic or technological affair of recycling machines and three R s.

Finally, it is worth stating that although schools may want to brag about using the latest technology for protection of the environment through waste management and recycling, it need not do a symposium on this.

Quexaminations

Dear Principal,

Examinations have been something, which have always bothered me in one way or the other. Why do we have examinations? Exams help to gauge if whatever knowledge and information has been given to the students has been assimilated or not. Or, let me put it this way...to know what the children learnt. Can there be a way to evaluate what students have learnt without asking them questions?

Why not evaluate a child on the basis of what he wants to know rather than what he knows? After all, if we call him a learner...we should evaluate him on the basis of how keen is he to learn rather that how much he has learnt. Can an examination be conducted with students asking questions instead of giving answers?

To The Principal
Yours sincerely

The basic problem that arises is how to evaluate a person on the basis of a question. It is difficult to do, but not impossible. And here we have to prioritise our purpose of education – do we want to evaluate a child on the basis of what he knows or do we also want to gauge what he may know, or rather, wants to know?

So why cannot a child write examinations (or whatever we may wish to call them), where s/he just writes what s/he wants to know? The child writes all the questions which come to his/her mind about the subject. And then the role of the teacher is not to mark his/her answer sheet, but to evaluate the quality of his/her questions and give answers back to that child. And the assessments would mark the child according to the how challenging the questions that have been put down.

Give the power back to the child – after all, s/he is the learner and unless the power is in the hands of the learner, s/he cannot learn. Society as a whole can decide on what it wants to educate its children about – but it is up to the child to learn that and move on.

To The Principal
Yours sincerely

The purpose of education is not children reproducing existing knowledge but children acquiring skills and knowledge to ask questions, which will help in the evolution of the existing body of knowledge.

A true educator will agree that what we want from children is not answers but questions. Then what one learns

To The Principal
Yours sincerely

can never be forgotten. If one forgets something, one never truly learnt it in the first place. All the effort to actually make children reproduce what they have learnt is worthless because even if they do so, there is no guarantee that they have learnt it.

Consider your own life. You may have reproduced the gospel truth in your examinations but ask yourself honestly – how much of it do you remember today? The answer would vary between 10% and 40%. Barely pass marks. If I say I always speak the truth…and write it…does it guarantee that I always speak the truth? No. Whatever remains is whatever is in the mind. And that is the truth.

We need to find what the child wants to know. This can be discovered by making the child submit questions instead of answers. We could tweak this a little bit and add, 'What do I know?' The power should be with the child to say and write what s/he has learnt. So, we may not require a question paper but just an answer sheet. After teaching three chapters, if the teacher wants to evaluate the students, she just needs to give a sheet to the children and ask them to write whatever they have learnt and how it has helped them.

To The Principal
Yours sincerely

I call the above 'Quexamination' – an examination where a child writes what s/he has learnt and writes questions about what s/he wants to learn about.

I can see fuming academicians here; it is just an experimental idea which could be piloted. At least some of the classes from grades 4 to 8 could experiment with this idea for one of their term examinations. There may be some wonderful results from this exercise.

A Quexamination would also fulfil another major objective of an 'examination' – to find the areas which the student needs to work upon. The student would spell out what s/he wants to know. It would also promote honesty in children. There would be no preparation required for this test. There would be minimal weightage for what the student knows and more weightage for what s/he wants to know.

If this experiment were to be taken forward, I understand it may be difficult for us as a society to grade and categorise students. There is one wild idea I have.

To The Principal
Yours sincerely

In Grade 12, each student writes a book. We call it the School Experience Book. This book would be the child's summary of what he has learnt in school and what he considers important from school education. It would contain all the knowledge the child thinks is important, which s/he learnt at school. It would have photographs, poems – anything the child wants to put into the book. It would be the Bible (no religious connotations) of that person. It could run into more than 100 pages. In this book, s/he also notes down what s/he wants to do further in life. S/he has to make a case for a career in that field. Why and how do they consider themselves fit for that branch of education? They also include questions they want to further explore in life.

Obviously it would take a lot of time to evaluate this book. So, perhaps we need to set up two CBSEs – i.e. CBSE 1 and CBSE 2. They work in alternative years so that they have a complete year to evaluate the School Experience Books.

This would also give a break of a year to the children – a concept I have mentioned in another chapter. After a year's break, a national board examines the books and decides on percentages and grades. It gives a recommendation for that child on some set parameters which s/he can use for his/her professional education. Professional colleges would then place half the weightage on the CBSE recommendation and the other half on their own test.

The above experiment leaves a lot to be created by the children and empowers them to reflect and take decisions on their choice of career. It is not difficult to evaluate a child on a report. While it may sound quixotic, if we really want children to lead meaningful lives, it is necessary to look at such alternatives. After all, the Armed Forces look at a 6-day interview with psychological, physical and academic components, as compared to other professions. Why then can we not look at something more meaningful as an evaluation for the school system? It would definitely be worth it. Although it is a difficult exercise to manage, it is certainly do-able. Perhaps, it requires another book to examine this new system? Nevertheless, it is high time schools started experimenting with new forms of examinations or quexaminations at least from Grades 3 to 8, which are considered the 'safe classes'.

To The Principal

Yours sincerely

With the advent of CCE, it may very well be possible for children to give examinations in variable formats. This format of quexaminations could be used in a FA. While the idea seems utopian, we could at least experiment with having a question paper in which the last question is: Please write questions about what you would like to know on the subject.

Professor Harbans Mukhia, a world renowned historian, taught Medieval History at Jawaharlal Nehru University (JNU), New Delhi and is now retired. His question paper was the most unusual I have ever seen. While the question paper was in the usual format with 6 or 7 questions, what was unusual was the end, where he stated: 'If you don't like any of the questions above, please create your own question and answer it'. Some of us actually did that. All he would do is distribute the question paper and disappear for two hours…come back and collect the answer sheets.

Education for Sustainable Development

Dear Principal,

Generations of chief guests and keynote speakers have spoken at school events and said that children are the future of this country and hence schools are actually building the country. They often speak about children changing India and making it a developed nation.

While I do believe that the present school children will make this country, I doubt if they will ever change the country or make India a developed nation. There is a strong argument behind this doubt. Our schools teach Maths, Science, English, Hindi and Social Studies (primarily). Within these subjects, two are languages – the medium of instruction. Among the other subjects, only Maths and Science are considered primary subjects and Social Studies

To The Principal
Yours sincerely

is considered as nothing but general knowledge about civics, geography and history.

For a child to change the country, s/he not only needs to be good in these subjects, but also needs to use these subjects to bring about development. But these subjects are not at all related to development. So, schools are churning out brilliant mathematicians and scientists (read engineers), but not people who can solve this country's problems. Interestingly, everybody would agree that India's problems are social in nature rather than scientific.

Studying Maths and Science helps you get good jobs so that you have a good standard of living – and we are getting that. The middle class are now living well. But they do not have a clue about how to solve the country's problems. All that they can do is crib about the corruption in the country, write articles and books. That is what school taught them…to write answers and not do anything. They cannot solve problems. The managers can achieve corporate targets but cannot meet the basic expectations of the country…to vote. This will continue to happen, as will the speeches of chief guest,

To The Principal
Yours sincerely

until schools start connecting children to the problems of the country.

Most schools try to cocoon the children from this country's problem and just show them clean and good places. There is no effort to connect them to the real India, with its problems – and let them take on a few.

To The Principal
Yours sincerely

This is the space where Education for Sustainable Development (ESD) comes in. ESD is primarily seen as environment education in quite a few quarters, but most people overlook the social and economic dimensions of ESD. For a developing country like India, ESD is the way to go. While Sustainable Development has a contested and varied definition, it may be worthwhile for schools to at least connect children to the country's problems and let them form their own meaning of sustainable development.

UNESCO is currently celebrating the Decade for Education for Sustainable Development (DESD) and it would be good if more and more people could be part of it. Let the children of a school identify a problem they want to work on. That problem could be anything ranging from corruption to bad roads. Let the students figure out what they want to do about it under the guidance of a facilitator. Let them go to government offices and figure out solutions for themselves rather than being confronted with its reality only when they get out of school.

Schools will have to actively empower students to find solutions to the country's problems. Possibly, apart from

To The Principal
Yours sincerely

the Roll of Honour for the best board results, there could be a roll of honour for the child who found a solution to a community problem or made a change. Because this country probably requires people to take the reins rather than just sit on a Roll of Honour.

Look at how most people in India feel disempowered about how this country is run and its problems. All we do is talk about it but cannot take action. The reality is that our education system, especially the school, has not taught us how to deal with it. It has equipped us to write and talk, and that is what we do.

Another reality is that while most adults feel that it is all a vicious circle and we cannot make changes, students do think otherwise. Given a chance to relate to the problems, they can work wonders.

Coming back to the original argument on sustainable development, our curriculum needs to clearly state how science can solve this country's problems. Our science textbooks need to include inventions from across the country – how people reinvented cycle rickshaws, *atta chakkis* or

To The Principal

Yours sincerely

started a blog or Facebook community for a developmental cause. Little boxes in our textbooks about all these things would be enough for the time being. Perhaps we need more deliberations from academic experts on this.

I remember being at a regional science exhibition at a school where Prof. Yash Pal was the chief guest and on the panel of judges. As usual, in the school science exhibitions, there were assembled kits which children had bought, with all kinds of jazzy electronics. And in one of the rooms stood two children who had created a very simple device for flushing. Their argument was that at public toilets, no one wants to flush because the flush handles are dirty. They created a device with which one could flush tapping one's foot (just like one opens a dustbin with the foot pedal). That device, though pretty archaic in front of hundreds of other exhibits, took my fancy and I hoped it would win a prize. It was a practical scientific solution to a public problem. Considering Prof. Yash Pal was on the panel of judges, it did indeed get the first prize. That is the way to go and that is science which can truly change this country and is related to its development. That is the science we need.

To The Principal
Yours sincerely

This is what education for sustainable development is all about. We need more ESD in the social sciences and the sciences domain as a developing country. It is the way to the future.

The 'Participatory' School

Dear Principal,

While participatory methodologies are much talked about by pedagogues and teacher trainers, the extent of their application is limited to doing participatory activities with students. So, there is a significant amount of participatory learning taking place in the classroom but the learning for the teacher is limited. Just like the children, participatory learning is important for the teacher as well.

For participatory learning of teachers to happen in school, teachers need to sit together, which they never get to do. In teachers training, the trainers involve participation only for what the trainers want to achieve. In staff meetings, the only things discussed are logistical matters – house duties, roles and responsibility. Just as I mentioned the conversations in the Principal's Office, the conversations, when the entire teacher body of the school gathers, are mostly logistical and administrative.

To The Principal
Yours sincerely

'Learning' is rarely discussed in such congregations. Such gatherings are perhaps the best places to create participatory learning in schools. How about the entire school staff gathering and discussing how the delivery of Maths could be made interesting? Teachers could sit in groups and decide on ideas. These ideas would be much more workable than those forwarded by the teacher trainers, who are usually not an intimate part of the school action. There is so much experience resting amongst teachers that if they are made to sit together in groups, they could come up with wonderful ideas which are actually implementable.

There could be monthly discussions taking up each subject and giving ideas. Apart from core subjects, imagine a discussion among the entire school staff to make the library an interesting place. It is interesting to note that an art teacher is as oblivious of Maths as a Maths teacher is of Art. They are just like students and can provide access into the blind spots of a subject teacher. After all the school is a family and its members can give suggestions to each other.

This participatory process in the school can work wonders with the school atmosphere and the change will be there for everyone to see.

Taking the participatory approach further, I have often wondered about the results of the children of this

To The Principal
___
Yours sincerely

country drawing their own NCF or National Curriculum Framework. Technically, society decides on what needs to be taught to children and in what way. But how would it be if the children, let us say Grade 5 or above (who have seen what society has to offer), sit together and decide what they want to learn and how?

This exercise could take place in each school of the country based on certain broad themes. Schools could later meet in clusters and regional conferences and deliberate on the same themes…and onwards to a national meet. The final 20-30 page document of what has been created by the children could then be presented to the main body of NCF for consideration. Though offbeat, this exercise could give interesting insights, add value and perhaps alter altogether the way in which we see NCF.

It has often pained me to see that there is some exemplary work being done in schools across the country (what many people call best practices), which do not spread nor have they been put together. There are a number of government and non-governmental initiatives, which are landmarks, but still very few people know about them.

Moreover, there is that innovative teacher in a school, who had a bright idea and implemented it, say in the library. That idea remains within that school until somebody notices it or does something about it.

In this information age, there is perhaps a need to have a website which collates everything - a website which could be called the www.participatoryschool.org. The main page of this website could be a 2D version of a school, which you can enter. It would be like a real life tour of the school, walking in the corridors. It would be possible for a user to enter a classroom or a laboratory or the library. Teachers across India could use this website to share their innovative ideas on each aspect. So, if a school librarian sitting in a village near Sambhalpur in Orissa, has an idea, all that s/he needs to do, is go to the website, enter the 'school', go to the library and put his/her ideas there.

As access to the internet increases and the website becomes popular, this website could perhaps be the biggest participatory ideas bank ever. People could go out there and pick up ideas to be implemented in their school. Like the wikipedia, but it would have school as a context and multimedia apparatus giving the feel of a school. Interestingly, even children could use this website and enter their ideas.

In a school, even before framing the NCF, school children could form a body to give ideas to the teachers and the Principal about making libraries, labs and other places interesting. I know a number of schools have been experimenting on this but not fully, as students' ideas are not taken seriously. Digantar in Jaipur, is one example, where the students' body has been empowered to give suggestions and implement ideas forwarded by the students. Perhaps, we need to emulate such examples.

While the pedagogues and professors of education have written books and spoken exhaustively on school education, it is high time we also listen to the teacher and the child and give respect to their ideas by promoting participatory schools - schools, which listen to and respect the ideas of the school community.

Let me share a personal experience which perhaps speaks volumes about how we hardly give space to our teachers to share ideas or listen to them. I also happen to be a teacher trainer. Modern teacher trainers usually give space to teachers to speak during trainings but with the rider that the sharing has to match the objective of the training. So, if the training is on higher order thinking skills, the teacher is bound to share ideas only around it. After a teacher has shared his/her ideas, the trainer speaks his own words of wisdom on the same. The rest of the time the trainer talks about some pedagogic fundamentals, which nobody seems to be interested in.

In a couple of my trainings, I decided to start the concept of a 'hot seat'. Once in the hot seat, the teacher is expected to share some story from his/her personal life about education and a piece of information about his/herself which nobody knows about. The teacher takes centre stage and the trainer joins the rest of the teachers.

While it was difficult for some to start off, in no time it became clear that apart from the classroom, the school had not given a platform for teachers to share. The stories that emerged were so interesting that they actually added a lot of value to the entire training. In fact, I have done it in all my trainings after that; there has not been a single training where I did not have teachers sharing their life experiences. This became a pattern and I realized that there is so much within a teacher that nobody listens to.

It is time the Principal listens to the teacher. While the Principal may be the leader and has the responsibility of the entire school, it is time to make the responsibility collective and participatory.

Acknowledgements

I have been contemplating writing a book for a long time. My Dad had been persuading me to live up to the family tradition of writing started by my grandfather, B.R. Musafir, who also gave the out-of-the-world surname to all of us – Musafir. It was the pen name or *takhallus* of my grandfather. So Dad, here you are.

My wife, Beas, an avid reader, had to take the pain to go through all the chapters of this book. In fact, she is the first person to read the book. Thanks for the effort.

My Mom for sharing her school days with me and my brother, Sandeep for getting me in touch with other authors. My mother-in-law, who read my first chapters.

Special thanks to my friend Deepali Jain and my ex-boss Sumita, for providing me with feedback on some chapters.

My friends, Osama Zaid Rehman and Ramachandran – from the publishing world, who have been with me in the journey to getting the book into print.

To The Principal
Yours sincerely

My office colleagues, Amita Bambawale, Aanchal and Jharna De, who were as excited about this book as I was.

How can I forget Pravah, the organization, which initiated me into education. My school friend Sriram Nathan, who gave me one of the first discourses on education. Did my journey actually start there?

And finally, Rustam Vania...the great artist who brought life to this book.

About the Author

Shankar Musafir graduated from H.P. University, Shimla, and then went on to do his Masters in History, and M.Phil (IR), from J.N.U, New Delhi. He presently works in the domain of school education with Indus World Schools.

Shankar originated the *Millennium Education for Sustainable Development Programme* (MESDP), which creates unique learning projects for children on developmental issues. He also created the internationally acclaimed *Kabadiwala* project which saw a *kabadiwala* as chief guest in a school. He continues to be an innovative teachers' trainer, having trained more than 5000 teachers across India and internationally. He is a keen writer on educational and environmental issues, an avid blogger, as well as an amateur film maker, trekker and cook.

This is Shankar's first book. He strongly believes that he does not remember even five percent of what he read in

To The Principal

Yours sincerely

school, college and university and that, apart from linguistic communication, formal education has not helped him in delivering his professional and other commitments. Whatever he has learnt has been through personal interest and experience. This realization has been the foundation of his work in the area of creative and practical education methodologies and content, for modern children and teachers alike. Shankar Musafir can be reached at: **smusafir@gmail.com**